Read

Preparing for Interview Questions on Your Job Search Journey

The One Hour Handbook Series

by

Dr. Staci McIntosh

This is a work of nonfiction. Nonetheless, some of the names and personal characteristics of the individuals involved have been changed in order to disguise their identities. Any resulting resemblance to persons living or dead is entirely coincidental and unintentional.

Copyright © 2017 Staci McIntosh

Published in the United States by Sensible Solutions
Henderson, Nevada

ISBN-13: 978-1-5220329-5-3

About the Author

Staci McIntosh has nearly 20 years of experience as a Human Resources executive in both public and private sectors. She has interviewed or coached over 1,000 individuals. Most have been just like you, wanting to perfect their skills for their next career move.

Staci writes her books with one goal: helping all people get the job they want. Through her brief, easy-to-read *One Hour Handbook Series,* she provides ambitious, hard-working people like you with useful tips you've probably never heard before. Staci knows her information will help you get your next job, because it's already worked for hundreds of others!

Staci entered the workforce as a teacher. She spent most of her career in the education field, eventually becoming an assistant superintendent and Chief Human Resources Officer. She then moved to the private sector. She is currently the Vice President of Human Resources for a popular casino resort on the Las Vegas Strip. Staci has a Bachelor's degree from Eastern Washington University, a Master's degree from Whitworth University, and an educational doctorate in leadership from Washington State University.

Staci lives with her husband Jim in Henderson, Nevada. Together they own Sensible Solutions, a consulting company devoted to providing practical resources for busy organizations and people. They enjoy eating great food on the Strip, binge-watching TV series, traveling, and spending time with Jim's teenage son Ben (an expert level Xbox One player) and Staci's daughter Kendall (a busy human resources professional).

To Jim, for loving me and for supporting my writing.
Without you, this book would never have been written.

And to my daughter Kendall, for making me so proud every day.

Table of Contents

Introduction

Two days before writing this, a young woman sought my advice on an upcoming interview. By all accounts, she was successful. At a young age, she was already a manager. She was on pace to finish her college degree in a few months. She had been highly recommended for this promotion by her previous supervisor. And yet, in her own words, she was "freaked out." Not by the fear of being unemployed. She had a job already. She was panicking that she might not do well. She worried that her unfinished degree would concern the interview team. She thought her experience would be rejected when stacked up against other candidates. Her inner critic was telling her she was inarticulate, dumb, and inexperienced. She imagined the interview team questioning why she had even applied for the promotion.

I asked her, "Do you have a voice in your head telling you you're not good enough?" She nodded and wiped the tears spilling over her eyes. Over the course of my career, I have seen this phenomenon many times. Sometimes the most qualified people go into interviews believing they are lacking and "less than" the competition. Sometimes the least qualified people are able to get an interview and then manage to land the job. How do the successful ones do it? Unless they are among the few people who were born with natural interview skills, they know how to prepare. Along the way, someone taught them, usually a mentor or a parent or a more experienced friend.

Here's the problem with most interview advice. People will tell you, "You need to prepare! You have to practice!" Very few people tell you exactly what that means. This book is different.

1

This book will give you detailed, step-by-step instructions about what real interview preparation means. I know it works because I've coached countless job seekers with the same advice. I've personally used it myself. I guarantee you that the easy to follow advice will help you at any step in your career ladder. If you're a student seeking your first job. If you're a front-line worker wanting to be a supervisor. If you're a stay-at-home parent or retiree returning to work. If you're a new leader wanting to move up, or an experienced leader wanting your dream job.

In Chapter One, I explain why you need to prepare. In Chapter Two, I tell you how to start preparing before you even have an interview. I give you strategies to anticipate the questions you'll be asked in Chapter Three. Chapter Four will tell you how develop robust answers that are both clear and concise. After reading Chapter Five, you'll find out how to rehearse the answers you developed. In Chapter Six I explain different interview formats you should anticipate. Finally, I give you the McIntosh Fifteen in Chapter Seven. These are the fifteen most commonly asked questions you will almost always get asked in one form or another when you begin to interview.

Adhere to these steps, and you will experience success every time. Whatever you need, you're going to find it in this book. And if you don't find it here, email me at stacimcintosh23@gmail.com. I will be happy to answer your question, because it will help me add what readers need to future updates!

You will get the job you want. Do you have an inner critic telling you you're not good enough? As I told the young woman, that's bull*$#t. Let's silence that critic once and for all. Read on.

Chapter One

Why Preparing Is So Important

During a job transition, I interviewed for a chief bargainer position. I had plenty of experience bargaining, but my current role at the time didn't require it. I prepared, but I knew, based on the questions, that I hadn't done well. I didn't have the complexity of experience they wanted. I felt stupid, ashamed of my performance. It's the worst feeling in the world leaving an interview knowing you could have done better. Even worse when you're a human resources professional who should have known better!

When you interview, sometimes it feels like you're naked. You're letting the interviewer conduct a thorough examination and evaluation of your worth. It can be a stressful, soul-baring, scary experience. Even more so if you really need a job, or it's the promotion you've been wanting for years and know you deserve.

But it's an even worse feeling knowing you didn't have the courage to apply, to make a change. You're taking that step to apply. Congratulations! Not taking the risk because you're afraid to fail is a permanent decision. Taking the risk and failing is a temporary, though impactful, pain. Be proud of yourself on taking the chance. Congratulate yourself on wanting to do your best. Honor yourself by putting in the time you will need to prepare and practice. It will frequently seem like an uphill battle, but your time will be worth it.

If think you know already *why* you should prepare. If not, let me tell you. You prepare because you will have competition.

And you prepare because it might be the one chance you have to get a job. Maybe it's your dream job. Maybe you've run out of your savings. Maybe it's the promotion you worked so hard for. Mostly, however, you prepare because it helps quiet that inner voice that questions your worth. You prepare because you don't want to look unqualified or unworthy. And, you prepare because you don't want to feel like you missed your chance--and that you let yourself down.

Now that you know why, I am going to go into great detail about *how* to prepare. The step-by-step methods I use will guide you through specific strategies. These strategies will train your brain and your body to do well in the interview. Each step is important. Brain psychology tells us that if you mimic a high-stress situation before you're actually in it, you're going to perform at your best.

Here's an example to illustrate the point. One year my friend Irene decided on a New Year's resolution that we were both going to complete a half-marathon by the end of June. Irene began running four days a week, and did so for six months, right up until the race. I hate to run, so I didn't train at all. I did get on Weight Watchers and lost fifteen pounds, so I had a thin "runner's physique" (Or, at least it appeared so in the right kind of jeans.) I started meditating also, envisioning myself motivated to run. Who did better in the half-marathon? Irene, of course. Why? Because she prepared for the task of running by actually running.

Oh, and I never ran the marathon at all. It didn't matter how often I meditated about running. It didn't matter how thin I became. I wasn't going to complete that marathon unless I actually practiced doing what I would have to do on that day. Run. For a very long distance.

The same thing happens if you don't prepare correctly for an interview. You can think about it. You can meditate on it. You

4

can put on your interview suit and imagine yourself answering questions. But unless you actually know and practice what you're going to say, you're going to be less prepared. And you're likely to fail, just like I failed at running a marathon.

Do you think Miss America just shows up the day of the pageant and says, "Gee, I wonder what that impromptu question is going to be! Hope it's something I know about!" No. She doesn't. She anticipates what the questions might be. She knows her answers to various topics, and she practices out loud. The same is true for politicians and public figures and anyone else frequently in the news.

Have you ever seen a spokesperson or politician interviewed by multiple media outlets on the same topic? They begin to sound like a broken record, using the same eloquent sound bites over and over again. You can be sure that in advance, they had a general idea about what questions they were going to get. And they knew exactly how they were going to answer them. You practice by *doing* because when you do the exact activity you're preparing for, you will do better. Visioning, positive self-talk and thinking about your answers will all certainly help. But all of those activities are not enough.

Interview Selection Process

By the time you get to the interview, you are competing with people who are similarly qualified, perhaps in different ways. All the time I hear the complaint, "I can't believe they hired so and so when I'm so much more qualified!" Here's a reality check if you have ever felt that way. Technically speaking, you were *both* equally qualified to receive an interview. Your experience level may be different from his, even more than his, but his personality may make him the better match for the position.

When you're selected for an interview, you're in a group of several people a hiring manager decided could do the job. One person's experience or education level might be higher than another's. But after the paperwork was reviewed, the hiring manager determined you were all similarly qualified to be successful. Even if it looks as if someone received an interview because of his social networks, a hiring manager decided he could do the job.

There is a difference between meeting minimum qualifications and being similarly qualified. If you don't meet the minimum education or work qualifications listed on the job posting, your application generally won't even get a review. Similarly qualified means that all applicants met the minimum qualifications. Thus, all are now eligible for further steps in the process. Now the selection process is about finding the one person who has the perfect mix of skills, personality and potential for success. You want to show the hiring manager that you are that one perfect match.

Beating the Competition

How does a hiring manager determine if someone has the perfect mix of skills to do a great job? Sometimes we get referrals. Sometimes we do a more thorough review of each resume or job application. Sometimes we conduct screening interviews with larger groups of applicants. But it all ends up at the same place: a final interview to see who gets the job. And at that point, how you present yourself is going to determine whether or not you get the job. Not your resume. Not your experience. Not your education. Not who referred you. At that point, it's all about the interview.

Once you're selected for that final interview, it becomes more about your interview performance than your minimum qualifications. You must prepare for that performance. It's partly about the chemistry between you and the interview team. It's also about how you represent the quality of your experience. At the interview, it's rarely about the actual years of experience.

You want *your* work history, whatever it is, to be judged the most applicable to the job. You want *your* answers to be the clearest. You want *your* personality to be likable without being obnoxious. Should you be yourself? Of course! Just be the most articulate, organized, and prepared version of yourself. That way, your experience, qualifications, and personality will shine through and wow the interview panel.

Take the Shortcut

1. The best way to learn how to interview well is to practice doing exactly what you will be required to do in the interview.

2. Once you get to the interview, your education and experiences won't matter as much as how well you present yourself.

3. To beat the competition, you have to be the most articulate, organized and prepared version of yourself so that your experiences and your personality shine.

Chapter Two

Start Preparing Before You Have an Interview

The strategies I'm going to give you throughout the rest of this book will require an investment of your time. I know you're committed to preparing, which is why you bought this book. You've made a great first start! As promised, it will be a quick read, and you can finish it within an hour.

The time it takes to truly practice for an interview in a way that will get you the job, however, is a lot longer. This is why it's important for you to begin preparing for an interview before you even have one. As soon as you start your job search, you can use my suggestions to start preparing.

In this chapter I'm going to share with you the best-kept secret weapon of the job search process, one you can use even before you see a job posted. It's easily accessible and full of information you'll need. I'm going to tell you where you can find it, why it's so important, and how it will help you to prepare for your interview. Using this secret weapon wisely and thoughtfully will instantly place you ahead of the competition.

Your Secret Weapon

The job posting (sometimes called job announcement or position description) is an often-neglected piece of important information. This is the secret weapon you will use to prepare for your interview. People disregard it for a variety of legitimate reasons. One reason is that job postings are notorious for being outdated.

However, go to Indeed or Monster and take a look at any of the hundreds of postings that are similar to the type of work you're looking for. This review will help you discover the skills that the type of job you're looking for will require. Even if you haven't applied to a specific position, job descriptions for similar positions will help you prepare well in advance of getting an interview. With technology having evolved, most large employers attach their job posting or job description to the on-line posting. It is quite easy to click on it and print it.

The job posting for the specific job you want gives you the minimum qualifications for the position. For example, say the minimum qualifications state you must have a Bachelors degree for the exact job you want. You don't have a Bachelors degree. So it doesn't make sense to apply, unless it's a job area where there is a shortage. You'll know that it might be a shortage area if the employer adds *or equivalent work experience* to the degree requirement.

The job posting will usually tell you how willing the company is to accept people who don't have the direct experience in the job posted. If it says, *Must have human resources or other similar operational experience*, that tells you something. They want someone with human resources experience. But they would accept someone who has *Other similar operational experience.*

What does that mean? That's the point. You don't know, and neither does the employer. When you see a posting with this wording, it's likely that the employer isn't sure there will be enough direct human resources candidates in the pool. Therefore, they want to cast a wide net and see who applies.

Most job postings will also tell you exactly the type of work you will be doing, listed under *Responsibilities*. These are the tasks and expectations the employer will expect you to have done or at least be familiar with. Job postings also tell you the type of skills they want you to have, listed under *Skills* or *Qualifications* or *Competencies*. These are usually broad skills or traits that aren't necessarily directly related to the job. For example, the qualification, *Ability to lead others while working as a member of a collaborative team* could apply to most any supervisory job.

Sometimes the job posting only gives a one-paragraph description, or just a simple listing of responsibilities. This tells you one of two things. It may be that the employer is open to a variety of candidates, which also means you'll probably have a lot of non-traditional competition. But it could also mean it's a small company with few human resources staff to create job posting details.

Whatever the case, gather all the information you can from the job posting. Imagine you're the person who wrote the description. What clues can you find about the type of person they are looking for? For example, I pulled a sales manager position from Indeed, one of my favorite job posting sites. Here's what the company has stated they want. From what they've written, what experiences and qualifications would their ideal candidate have?

About Us: We provide a comprehensive solution for liquid waste collection, processing and compliance for all types of waste generators. From grease to grit, lint to municipal sludge and food wastes to septic; we can meet all non-hazardous liquid waste transportation needs. Unlike most, we also boast proprietary disposal facilities in most major markets we operate in. Fully permitted and staffed with trained professionals, our customers can be confident in the handling of their waste materials.

Job Description: Incumbent must be able to generate revenue utilizing a consultative selling approach in the sale of our services to a wide range of potential accounts. Candidate will be responsible for prospecting and closing business to achieve sales revenue goals in a defined sales territory.

Essential Duties and Responsibilities include the following, but are not limited to:

- *Manage prospects by developing sound marketing plans and maintaining key information in the sales tracking database.*
- *Meets or exceeds sales call activity goals for new sales.*
- *Proposes customer solutions that are compliant with appropriate local and state federal regulations.*
- *Matches customer's needs with company services.*
- *Effectively communicates pricing and service strategies to both external and internal customers.*

- *Job Requirements:*
- *Bachelor's degree, or;*
- *Minimum 5 years service related sales experience in lieu of a Bachelor's degree.*
- *Phone based business to business (B2B) prospecting resulting in successfully obtaining customer appointments is highly preferred.*
- *Previous liquid or solid waste removal sales experience highly desired.*

Now that you have in mind what this employer wants, take one side of a piece of paper and draw a line down the middle. On the left side, write the responsibilities (work), competencies (skills) and any personality traits you can identify from the posting.

I would write things like this:
Knows waste management (solid or liquid)
Can solicit new customers in person over the phone
Consults with potential customers to identify their needs
Helps customers solve their waste problems
Can understand and adhere federal and state regulations

11

Knows how to explain pricing options
Can hit sales targets and goals
Bachelor's degree or five years of sales/service experience

On the right side of the paper, begin listing the experience you have that relate to each of the qualities the company wants. It doesn't need to be direct, full-time work experience. It could be volunteer experience, community involvement, or part-time work.

In addition, the company has broadly defined the experience to include sales jobs where you solved a problem for the customer while selling them a product. Direct experience is always best, but closely related experience may get you an interview if they don't have a lot of candidates. Think to yourself, how many people actually have experience in *solid and liquid waste management?*

Now that you've gathered the information from the posting, it's time gather as much information as you can about the company.

Researching the Company

Ideally, before you apply for any job, you'll have researched the company thoroughly. If you wrote a cover letter when you applied, hopefully you will know enough about the company to have included some of the information in the letter. *(For more information, see my book Job Search Passport: Using Industry Secrets to Write Applications, Resumes, and Cover Letters.)*

But sometimes you're so busy applying for jobs that you don't have time to do the type of research that is required to prepare for the interview. When you research a company, look for any information that helps you to understand the qualities of the people they have hired in similar jobs. The company website itself is a great way to learn about the organization's size, business, and goals. Look for characteristics that match your own background. Continue the list you began on the right side of your paper. This time, write down all of the experiences you've had that relate to the information you discovered about the company.

If the company's business is completely outside of your experience in every way, write down important information, but put it on the left side of your paper. Highlight it so that later you can remember to think of a way to address that gap when preparing your answers.

On most company websites, you can find a *Careers* tab at the top or the bottom. Click on that to find out more about the company's mission. For example, Urban Outfitters states on its career page:

Today, Urban Outfitters has over 200 stores in the United States, Canada and Europe, offering experiential retail environments that combine a curated mix of women's, men's, accessories and home products with an eye toward creativity and cultural understanding. The idea of Urban Outfitters' being a place for likeminded creative individuals and as a creation of community spaces continues today. We share our customers' interests and values, representing community at all times by offering inclusion in social media, events, community involvement, and entrepreneurial opportunities.

From this description, you might write in your left column that they are looking for someone who knows about multiculturalism. They want someone who is creative. They value someone who has been involved in his community. If you had any experiences related to those characteristics, you would write those notes on the right side of the paper.

You'll also want to find out what type of people your potential employer typically hires. I think LinkedIn is one of the best ways to research the backgrounds of people who have been hired by that company. Type the company name and the job category in the search field, then begin clicking on the profiles of people who have the type of job you'll be interviewing for. (Be sure to change your viewing mode to anonymous before clicking on profiles.)

This time, you're looking for trends. This will give you valuable information about what you might want to emphasize in the interview. It will also give you a realistic look at who your competition might be. The key is to focus on the trends you see that relate to your own experience. Similarities in charity work, outside interests, or type of industry constitute a potential win for you during the interview.

Cyberstalking the Panel

When you receive communication to schedule you for an interview, find out as much as you can about the interview length and the people interviewing you. You can do this by saying (or emailing) something like, *Thank you so much for the opportunity to interview! Are you able to let me know how long I should plan for the interview, and whom I will be meeting with?* If the person scheduling tells you he/she doesn't know, or has to get back to you, then you cheerfully say, *Ok, that's fine!*

That said, normally the scheduler will be able to tell you who will be interviewing you. Write down the names. Then get to work on LinkedIn. I want to be very clear. The purpose of finding out information about interview panel members is NOT to make it obvious you have stalked them on LinkedIn or Facebook. Rather, the purpose is to find similarities to your background. Unconsciously, panels tend to hire people who look and sound like themselves. As a result, people who are similar to the panelists are more likely to be hired. This pattern can foster discriminatory hiring practices if panels aren't educated to avoid the tendency to hire those just like themselves.

However, no matter what your background is, you can overcome this tendency by being strategic about your answers and your comments before and after the interview. The similarities you find can be related to work experience. They can also be related to personal interests. Continuing down the left side of your divided paper, write down the panelists' names with their interests. On the right side, note any similarities to yourself.

As you think about the interests you share in common with the panelists, be sure you're being totally honest. You're not going to casually mention a marathon you're running in a month if your normal routine is walking on a treadmill. You're also not going to insert comments into the interview that might indicate you did in fact cyberstalk the panelists. You will only use honest information that comes up naturally in the conversation.

I was on one interview where it was very clear the candidate had thoroughly researched each panelist's Facebook page. It felt creepy when she shook each person's hand and said, "Oh I know you. I love your dogs! I have two dogs just like that!" She had a comment for EVERY panelist. I applaud her initiative, but the way she implemented it failed.

On the other hand, once a prominent community member was interviewing me. He had no social media presence, so I had researched him on the internet using a simple Google search. I found very old news clipping which stated he had been instrumental in stealing my former hometown's local baseball team and moving them to his own city. In the small talk before the interview, I jokingly referred to the incident, telling him, "I won't hold it against you!" I found out later he was very impressed that I took the time to find out such an obscure fun fact.

15

Keep writing down all facts, experiences, and interests you can find about the company and the panelists. In the next section, I'll provide more detail regarding what you'll do with the information.

Think Like a Matchmaker

Now you have a sheet of paper divided down the middle. On the left side are traits the company wants, values of the company, and characteristics of the panel. On the right side, you've briefly noted similarities to your own qualifications and background. Now it's time to think more intently about your specific experiences. These experiences will form the basis of your answers to interview questions.

You need to remember and write down as many details as possible about the experiences that relate to the job posting. On a separate piece of paper from the one you've been working on, this time create three columns. The left section will be called *What I did.* The middle section will be called, *What happened.* The right section will be called, *Traits I exhibited.*

Think back to at least one year ago from the time you're reading this book. Start with that month. Alternatively, you could go back to a month that makes the more sense because it was a transition in your career or life. For example, you might start with September, even though it was a year and a half ago, because that was the month you became president of a community organization. Or maybe you want to start with fifteen months ago because that was the year you were hired at your job. The key piece is that you are going to go month by month.

Most people, if they prepare at all for an interview, think about the big events or projects they've worked on. They fail to

16

include the important everyday successes they have experienced. People who tend to doubt themselves even focus on their perceived failures rather than their everyday performance.

By thinking carefully through each month, you are likely to remember more of your accomplishments. One major help to your interview preparation is taking the time once every three to six months to write down your work projects and successes for that time period. That way, you will have them handy just for this purpose.

Assuming you haven't done that, use this strategy to identify your everyday accomplishments. If you have a calendar, go through it to remind yourself of the meetings and activities you were focused on that month. Think carefully, reviewing calendar events or triggers that will help your memory. Big projects and successes are great. But this is a brainstorming activity where you write down all experiences.

You will list activities related to your time spent on paid work, community work, or even what you did as a stay-at-home parent organizing your kids, or volunteering at their school. You may not think it was important that you encouraged one of your coworkers who lacked self-confidence to approach the boss with a process improvement. But that is an example of you coaching and developing others, an important ability for a wide variety of positions.

Month by month, write down those activities in the left column. Be sure to include everything you can remember. Don't judge yet whether it was significant or not, and don't fill out the second and third columns just yet. At the end of a 20-30 minute brain dump, going month by month, you should have a fairly long list of activities. If you don't, you're probably overthinking it too much. If that happens, set it aside for a day. Then return to it, doing the same activity when your brain and sub-conscious have had some time to think of other activities.

After you have your long list in the left column, fill in the middle and right columns for each activity. In the example of you coaching a coworker, the *What I did* was encourage Bob to approach our boss with his suggestion about how we can save money by using a different supplier. *What happened* was that Bob shared his suggestion with the boss, the boss rejected his idea, and Bob came back to me mad. Then I gave him advice to not take it personally if his suggestions aren't implemented. *Traits I exhibited* were encouraging, coaching, and advising someone about how to work with others.

Continue to fill in the middle and right columns in this manner. You will begin to see that even the smallest events have the potential to provide an example of your work habits in a job interview. If you can't think of anything for the middle and right columns, skip them and go onto the next activity you listed. You want to keep brainstorming as many activities as possible.

Once you're done, it's time to think like a matchmaker. You have your job description, company information, and panelist information list. You've already filled in some of your experiences that match that list. Now review your new list of activities while looking at your original two-sided sheet. On your three-column brainstorming list, use a highlighter to identify when you see an activity that directly matches your position and company information.

If you have several interviews coming up, make multiple copies of the list for highlighting. Not all your experiences are going to match at least one qualification listed for a job, but many will. Keep copies of the comprehensive list. It will help you for future interview preparation as well.

Take plenty of time to develop this list. Also keep a running log of accomplishments when you're in any job. These two strategies will save you a lot work when it comes to interview preparation in the future.

Take the Shortcut

1. Use the information on the job posting to understand what the company is looking for and how your background and experience would match their needs.

2. Find out everything you can about the company and the type of people they hire by using free tools available on the internet such as the organization's career web page and LinkedIn.

3. Use LinkedIn and other social media resources to find out if you have similar connections and interests to those who will be serving on the interview panel.

4. After brainstorming your activities each month over the course of a year, decide which ones apply to the information you've gathered about the job expectations, the company, and the panelists.

Chapter Three

Anticipating Questions

This is an easy concept to understand. It's also an important one to put into practice. You need to write down the questions you think you might be asked. You won't guess correctly on all of them. You may have written down and practiced different questions from the ones you'll be asked. But the questions that *are* asked will most likely be similar enough that you'll be able to use your practiced answers.

Even if the questions aren't very similar, you will be extremely well-rehearsed when describing your examples. Whatever questions you use the examples for, you will be confident and eloquent.

Another reason to generate specific questions is that it prepares you psychologically. Many people prepare for interviews only by thinking of general topics. That helps, but it doesn't "rehearse" the actual event for your brain. As in my running example, it's like training to run a marathon by walking instead of running. Both may get you to the finish line in some fashion, but if you want to be proud of your performance, you need to run.

Where To Find Questions

Each time I give this advice, people want to know where and how to find questions that might be asked. For some, it's the secret world of corporate human resources, where only a lucky few can interpret the interview map. Not true. Remember the secret weapon? The job posting. It is going to be your first source of questions.

Take the job expectations, put a *Tell us about a time when you had to...* in front of each expectation and you have an interview question related to the job. Using our Waste Management Region Sales position, the job expectation says: *Proposes customer solutions that are compliant with appropriate local and state federal regulations.* That turns into an interview question that might look like this: *Tell us about a time when you've had to help a customer solve a problem while still keeping in mind local or state federal regulations.* Or the panel might ask the question a little more subtly: *What issues would you need to keep in mind when helping a customer solve a problem or meet a business objective?*

The topics contained in the job posting or position descriptions are going to drive many of the topics you'll encounter at the interview. But not all. Whatever job type you're looking at, conduct a Google search for that profession's questions. For example, let's say you're interviewing to be a cocktail server. You can actually find resources on the internet which will give you interview questions unique to that job type.

Writing this chapter, I tried to guess questions that might be asked of a cocktail server candidate. I guessed there would be questions about providing good customer service, dealing with irate guests, and juggling many orders at once. When I did the Google search, I found additional questions I wouldn't have anticipated. I hadn't thought about *You look overqualified; why do you want this job?* Yet it is a logical question that could be asked. Another was *Name five red wines, five brands of vodka, and five types of steak.* I had a few ideas initially, but the Google search gave me more questions to practice.

While Google searching questions can be useful, avoid using pre-scripted, pre-written answers. Blogs or books that give you interview questions and so-called right answers may seem tempting at first, but they are likely to hinder your interview. Assume that your competition may have read the same books. Your answers will be strangely similar. The interview team might wonder if you're using examples from your own experience. Further, if you've memorized answers that don't seem original or authentic, your interview style will be boring and uninspiring. You can gather a few ideas from the answers others provide. Just make sure your examples and thoughts are your own in order for you to succeed.

Another great place to get interview question ideas is from previous interviews! Every time you leave an interview, you should immediately write down the questions you were asked. Do it right when you get into your car or when you walk out of the room. You are likely to encounter similar questions in subsequent interviews. This is especially true if you're interviewing with the same company for different jobs. It is also true if you're interviewing within the same general job category. Writing questions down immediately will help you develop your own question bank for future use and will streamline your interview preparations in the future.

Finally, in Chapter Seven, I provide you with what I believe are the most common interview questions. I give you ideas for content as well as what mistakes to avoid when answering them. Most one-hour interviews will contain at least four or five of these questions in some version or another. Along with question content ideas from the job description, preparing for these fifteen questions will always ensure you are ready for almost every question asked.

Question Categories

In my experience interviewing others and researching new questions, I have found that questions tend to fall into four different categories. The first category contains two questions you will get 99% of the time. These questions are the easy ones and there is absolutely no reason why you should not answer them perfectly. At the beginning, the question is *Tell us about your background and experiences, and tell us why you want to work for us.* At the end of the interview, the panel will ask you if you have any questions, and then they will ask *Do you have anything you'd like to add (or) Is there anything we haven't asked you about that you think is important for us to know?*

You will always get some version of these questions, so prepare for them well. The opening question gives the interview panel a first impression of you. First impressions tend to linger throughout the interview. Make your first impression a good one. The final question will leave the panel with a lasting impression. It should make you stand out among several candidates in a long day of interviews.

The second category of questions relate directly to the information on the job description. I referenced these earlier in the book. You create them by turning the job responsibility into a question about your experience in that area. You can also find these questions via an internet search when you enter the type of your job and the word *interview questions*. For example, in the Google search I conducted, I entered *Interview questions & cocktail server.*

The third category of questions has the purpose of getting to know your personality traits or qualities. Most interviews will also contain a few questions in this category. You can answer these questions without having any direct experience in the job, so they are easy to prepare for. These are questions such as: *Tell us your strengths and weaknesses. What are your outside interests? Tell us something about yourself that would surprise most people to know. What is your leadership style?* As stated earlier, Chapter Seven contains more examples of questions that are in this category.

The fourth category of questions is "Creativity Probes". To an outside observer, these questions might seem wacky and unlikely to tell you that much about whether or not someone can do the job. Examples of these questions, pulled from the internet, are: *Would you rather fight one horse-sized duck, or 100 duck-sized horses? What would the name of your debut album be? If you were a brand, what would be your motto? You're sent to a deserted island and can bring only two items: a book and a tool. What book and what tool would you bring? If you could choose between two superpowers--being invisible or flying, which would it be?*

I have seen these questions used by companies with highly innovative, non-traditional work environments. Companies on the cutting edge of organizational innovation ask these questions in order to judge a candidate's ability to think and operate completely outside the norm. Sometimes they ask the question because the job requires the candidate to be comfortable handling non-traditional customers or thinkers. Many technology-oriented, innovation-producing organizations ask these questions to judge creativity, a person's ability to think quickly on his feet, and to gauge if the candidate would fit the culture and work environment.

When you get one of these questions, you should know that there is no right answer. The panel is judging your creativity and thought process, not whether you chose to be a sheep or a snake. You can't prepare for these questions in a traditional way, but you can be aware they might be asked. There are several career websites and articles that identify weird questions and the companies who have asked them. Do a quick internet search using the phrase, *Weird interview questions* and you will begin to see the general tone of these questions. At the very least, you can think ahead about how you will analyze the question before you answer.

By now, you have a long list of your own activities and experiences matched to your target organization's needs. You have written down questions that are likely to be asked. You have reviewed other questions that may be asked. Now it's time for you to organize your answers to those questions.

Take the Shortcut

1. Use the job posting or job description to generate probable questions.

2. The internet, as well as books which give sample interview questions, are valuable resources to prepare for interview questions.

3. Anticipate questions that will be related to the job responsibilities, and also anticipate those that will ask you about your personality traits or work style.

4. Be aware that some innovation-focused companies ask questions that may seem weird. These questions are designed to judge your creativity, thought process, and fit to that organization's work culture.

Chapter Four

Constructing Answers

This chapter is about how you are going to create coherent, organized answers that will impress the interview team. For those of you who remember writing class in school, you'll notice that the format isn't much different from writing a clear paragraph. You'll have a main point and then you'll have supporting examples.

In order to have clear, articulate answers in the interview, you're going to need to take the questions you've prepared for and actually write out answers to those questions. Focuses on the top twenty that you think are likely to be answered. Writing out your answers may take you a few hours to do, but it is well worth it. Once you've done it for any one job, you can easily adapt it to other interviews.

Begin by writing out the answers in paragraph, story-telling form as an initial start. Write them out just as you would answer them. Then read them out loud to see if what you've written matches your natural pace when you're talking. After you've done that, go back and create an outline with your main point and examples.

Some people choose to write the outline first. Then they write out the entire answer after that. You should use the method that best works for you. If you can go straight from an outlined answer into having a well-rehearsed response, go for it. I have found that most people need to write a paragraph in order to practice things like transitions and opening comments.

Philosophy and Specifics

As you begin to write down your possible interview answers, you have to avoid a mistake that many make. When asked an interview question, many people provide way too many philosophy statements. They don't give enough specific examples for the interview panel to believe that the candidate can put that philosophy into action. The panel wonders if the person is all talk and no action.

Other people make the opposite mistake. They provide specific examples. But then they don't share an overall belief or philosophy statement to bring the concepts together. The interview panel is left with a feeling of *So what?* They wonder if the candidate is just listing experiences without understanding why his actions were important.

In my experience, women tend to give more philosophy and men tend to give more examples. That's a generality, so you should reflect on what your tendency is. When you formulate your answers, be sure that you are giving specific examples as well as an overview or belief statement. This makes it clear to the interview team what you've done, what your viewpoint is, and how you think about work situations.

You may be wondering how to know if you're making either mistake. Any time you say something that is about a specific action you did or would do, that is a detail. If you are talking about something you believe or you're describing yourself or your approach, that is an overview or philosophy statement. Again, make sure your answers contain both.

Here is an example to help you understand the concept. Question: *How would you deal with an irate customer?* Answer A (heavy philosophy, few details): *I believe that it's important to stay calm myself and not get mad myself. Customers get mad, but if they believe they are being listened to, they are more likely*

28

to help us provide a resolution to their concern. I'm a pretty happy person, so a customer getting mad doesn't really bother me. I'm always able to solve their problems.

Answer B (heavy details, little philosophy): *I've had this happen a lot in my career. Once, the customer was mad because there were two extra drinks on his bill that he said he hadn't ordered. I believed he had ordered them. I didn't get mad. I listened and told the customer I would look into it. Then I got my manager and we agreed that it wasn't worth it and that we would just comp off the drinks. So then the customer was happy.*

Answer C (philosophy and details): *Of course there are always going to be customers who get mad about something. I believe when dealing with one who is irate, the most important thing is to be sure that the customer feels listened to, and that they feel like you're really working to solve the problem. I had a customer once who was mad because there were two extra drinks on his bill that he said he hadn't ordered. I knew he had ordered them, but I didn't argue with him, and I stayed calm. I listened, and then I told the customer I would see what I could do. Then I got my manager and we agreed that it wasn't worth it to have the customer leave angry, so we comped off the drinks and the customer left happy.*

You can see that answers A and B weren't too bad. They both might be completely acceptable. But acceptable isn't going to get you the job in a competitive environment. In answer A, the interview panel understands what the candidate says she would do. But they wonder if she would use that philosophy with an actual irate customer. She didn't give any specific experiences, so they don't know.

In Answer B, the interview panel sees that the candidate handled one situation correctly. But how does she think? Will she always request free food and drinks when a customer is

29

mad? The panel might guess at the philosophy driving her actions, but they don't know for sure because she didn't make it explicit.

Answer C gives the interview team the best insight regarding how the candidate thinks about customer problem-resolution and what she would actually do. It's clear that she understands the big picture regarding this part of customer service. It's also clear she has the background and specific experiences to show the interview panel that what she believes is how she would act on the job.

Ensure you are providing both philosophy and specifics when you answer each question. If you use this format, you will always answer any interview question fully and completely

Clarity and Organization

You've got your experiences listed. You've pondered how to include a belief or philosophy statement to summarize your viewpoint on each question. Maybe you've even taken an initial stab at writing out your answers. Now it's time to ensure your answers are organized. You want to make your answers clear to the interview team while seeming very natural.

If you've ever been on an interview panel, you probably had at least one candidate whose answers seemed disjointed and wandering. In those cases, the interview team states that they just don't get what the candidate said. They don't know what he meant, even though he provided some examples. If it was really bad, the interview team might conclude that they candidate is not even qualified for the job. If answers are disorganized and confusing to the panel, they conclude, *The experience on his resume must be inflated!* or *I just can't see her leading a team.*

When a candidate has a lot to say, but the sentences aren't organized in a way that makes sense to the audience listening, it will be difficult to get the job. When you're writing your answers out, imagine a triangle. You can start with the specifics at the point in the triangle and then conclude with your broad philosophy or believe statement. You can also start with a broad statement and then move into specifics.

What you absolutely cannot do is weave in and out of philosophy, examples, other broad statements, and other examples. It will confuse your audience. And it will pull your thought process off track.

Answering an interview question is the same as giving an impromptu speech on a topic you know only a little about. Pretend like you have to convince them of an argument and then organize your answers that way. When you outline your answers, they should have a clear format that's easy for the panel to follow.

Here are some various ways you might organize your answers. I have the broad topic or belief statement coming at the beginning, but in practice you will probably mix it up somewhat and put it at the end for some questions.

- Broad topic/belief statement. Example A. Example B. Example C.
- Broad topic/belief statement. Step 1, Step 2, Step 3.
- Broad topic/belief statement. Story example beginning. Story example middle. Story example end.
- Broad topic/belief statement. Example related to part A of the question. Example related to part B of the question.
- Broad topic/belief statement. Trait A description. Trait B description.

When I share this answer structure with people, I have to offer one disclaimer. You are not going to say, *My belief statement is* _____. *My examples to support that belief are* _____. Rather, the structure is happening behind the scenes and drives the order that you speak the sentences. You don't use the structure words in your interview answers.

I once had an aspiring school administrator take this advice very literally. Like you, she was committed to preparing. She listened intently to my advice. She attended two different seminars I provided. When she finally did get an interview, in each answer she provided, she referred to the structure when answering. Needless to say, it was very distracting and she did not get the job. (After further coaching she had one of the best interviews I've ever seen and is now a highly successful school principal.)

The structure of your answers should operate behind the scenes. When your structure is perfect, the interview panel will view you as naturally well spoken. More importantly, they will view your answers as on-point, robust, and full of information supporting you as the best candidate.

Take the Shortcut

1. Write out your full answers to the top twenty questions you think are likely to be asked in the interview.

2. Make sure each answer contains a broad statement that gives the interview panel insight into your beliefs and thinking.

3. Make sure each answer also contains specific examples from your experience so that the interview panel knows you will demonstrate what you believe by showing what you will do on the job.

4. Organize your answers into a clear structure that will be easy for the interview team to understand.

5. Don't refer to the structure itself when interviewing. Based upon your well-organized answers, the panel will simply view you as the most clear and well-qualified candidate.

Chapter Five

Rehearsal Steps

Rehearsing your answers isn't a matter of softly mumbling into the air what you think you might say. Rehearsing your answers involves several components. When you take the time to do them, you will feel more confident in the interview, which will be apparent to the interview team.

Equally important is that you will be judged as a clear, engaging speaker, which will put you ahead of the competition. I can always tell when I interview someone who has practiced versus someone who has not. People who have practiced may not do everything perfectly, but their personality shines through, and they always include multiple examples in their answers.

Memorize Main Points

Step one is to memorize the key points of your answers. It is exactly like studying for a test. You look at the notes you have on each anticipated question. You memorize the main point or belief statement. Then you memorize each component of your example.

Because you always know you're going to get the "Tell us about yourself" question, that answer should be perfectly rehearsed, just like you're giving a speech. The same is true for the questions you will ask the panelists at the end, as well as the closing statement. Your final statement should always be eloquent, so that it leaves the panelists with a good impression of who you are.

Practicing will take time, but you already wrote out the content. You prepared by generating multiple work examples. It won't do you any good in the interview if you can only remember two examples of the ten you wrote out. Candidates who have less work experience than others tend to do this. When that happens, interview panelists judge the candidate as not having enough experience to do the job.

Being sure you have your examples or sub-topics memorized avoids this problem. If it's been a while since you've memorized something at school, here's what you do:

1. Look at the first answer and read it.
2. Look away from the paper and memorize the main points.
3. Look at the second answer and read it.
4. Look away from the paper and memorize the main points.
5. Look back at the paper and quickly view questions one and two.
6. Look away from the paper and see if you can recall all of the main points from question one and question two.
7. Continue this process until you have all of the main points memorized.

Sometimes a word game helps you memorize the main points of the questions. What you do is create a word in which every letter represents the examples or sub-topics in each question's answer. For example, let's say you anticipated a question on teamwork like *What do you think are the most important components that help a team work together effectively?* Let's say your memory word is C.A.R.E. The C stands for a broad example: *The team has to <u>care</u> about each other's needs and work styles.* The A stands for a related, specific example: *When team members complete a task or contribute to the work, others show <u>appreciation</u> for what each* *individual has done.* The R stands for: *Team members* <u>respect</u> *each other's differences and use the differences to complete tasks efficiently.* The E becomes the summary or belief statement and stands for: *The outcome of any team effort should be really* <u>excellent</u> *work. Teams can have all of the traits I mentioned and get along, but unless their work is excellent, that goal hasn't been achieved.*

Your brain has a huge capacity to memorize facts. But your brain also likes to chunk longer thoughts together. When you use this memory strategy (it's called a mnemonic), you'll find that memorizing just that one word leads you to the one letter of the word. Then that one letter will trigger your brain into remembering your whole example.

Practice Out Loud

Once you're memorized your belief statements and examples for each question, it's time to start practicing you answers out loud. To do this, you need a paper just with the questions on it. You'll start by sitting down at a table and doing one full run-through of answering the questions out loud. No peeking at your written outline!

As you're answering the questions out loud, use a highlighter. Note the questions you didn't do well on. You'll highlight the ones that you completely missed, the ones you couldn't remember at all what you wanted to say. For those questions, go back to your outline and re-memorize. While you're there, take note of any examples or points you might have forgotten. Then go back to the table with just the questions and try again.

When you practice your questions out loud the first few times, you'll find out that other, and sometimes better, ideas come to your mind. You'll find that as you talk, further insights or eloquently worded statements magically come out of your mouth. That's how the brain works. When you're focused on something, your sub-conscious goes to work in the background and you get bursts of brilliance!

Use those moments and write down what you said. Then practice using the example the next time around. After all this work, you're in the home stretch. Hopefully, you started practicing interviewing well before you actually received an interview. If so, you probably have a few more days, if not more, to practice.

Even if you only have a day or two to practice, begin answering questions out loud whenever you can: in the car, while cooking dinner, during your morning walk or lunch break, while vacuuming, or during whatever activities you normally do throughout the day. The more you practice, the better likelihood you have of blowing the competition out of the water.

Refine Your Answers

As you've been practicing, you've been refining your answers along the way. Your brain stretches to bring in new information you hadn't yet thought about. Now it's time to take a more critical look at your answers to add a few key components that will make them even better. To be clear, these are refinements; they are not requirements. If you don't include them, but you follow the other advice in this book, you're going to do great. They are worth considering, though, as they will serve to impress the interview panel.

The first refinement is to add some humor. If you're not a naturally funny person, this may be difficult for you, so don't stress out over adding it. But if as you're practicing, you

37

naturally think to add a few funny comments, go ahead and use them in the interview. Just make sure that the humor is something that makes fun of yourself, or a general situation. Make sure it's appropriate and doesn't involve swearing or anything that might be viewed as mocking any one specific cultural, racial, or political group. Also make sure you're not putting down the company inadvertently.

For example in an interview for the sales position at that liquid and solid waste management company, it would not be advisable, for example, to say, even jokingly, *Wow, must be tough since you're basically selling a product dealing with people's shit.* However, it might be amusing to say, *I bet not everyone understands that if weren't for you guys, they would have big messes to deal with on their own!* If you're not sure if a line is funny or not, run it by some people you trust. Get their opinion regarding its use in an interview. And when in doubt, leave it out.

Another nice interview add on is to offer a unique viewpoint that shows you're current, knowledgeable, and interested in the type of job you're interviewing for. When you get to the interview point, as I've said before, you're on a very similar playing field compared to everyone else. You can bet that at least some of your competition has also been practicing answers to questions. On the panelist side, it gets really boring when every person says that their biggest weakness is *my need for perfection*. It's obvious everyone read advice that told them to have a strength as a weakness.

If you conducted research on your job-area topic, you might be able to say: *I know that marketing people in general have a weakness in the area of (insert from your new learning here). I think I've really worked to overcome that tendency by (insert more from your new learning).* When you weave in current ideas that represent new or emerging thinking in your area, it impresses the panel. You can do this whether you're interviewing for a managerial position or even a front-line position.

Let's say you're interviewing for a cook job at McDonald's. Impress the interview team by knowing something cool about new technology in the high-volume food production area. Google is your friend for this, as is Kindle unlimited. Through Kindle unlimited, you get to borrow up to 10 books at a time for $9.99 per month. It doesn't apply to all books, and most current best sellers aren't on the list. But it's worth the investment if you want some quick fun facts to weave into your interview.

Finally, if you're seeking a promotion into a job that might be a stretch for you, consider doing some outlier research on your topic. By this I am referring to new thinking, ideas, or research studies that are not currently in the mainstream of your work function. You can say: *I love (insert job area related topic) and some people are now saying that (insert how most people do or think about things) needs to be changed so that (whatever interesting opinion you found).* You can also review multiple books on the topic. Come up with your own conclusion, which will be even more powerful to use in an interview.

These are some ways you can add a little oomph to your interview content. Again, don't overthink it and don't add any of this content if it doesn't feel right. You need to be *you* in the interview. I also don't want you to look stressed trying to remember content that isn't coming naturally to you the way describing your own experiences will.

Get Uncomfortable

I bet by now you're getting pretty tired of practicing and repeating questions out loud. Your family could go to the interview, pretend to be you, and do fairly well based on the answers you prepared! For you, it's time to do a true dress rehearsal. For this step, you will put your body and mind through the exact same steps you will take during the interview. There are parts of your subconscious brain that will remember the rehearsal and will help you do even better on the big day.

Do your best to make the dress rehearsal a close approximation to what you'll experience when it's show time for real. Get dressed in your interview suit or outfit. If you don't have access to an empty office, then find the place in your house that you spend the least amount of time in. Sit yourself down at a table. Bring in a card table or coffee table if you have to. Place three or four friends or family members around the table. Now, conduct your dress rehearsal.

Each of your group will take turns asking you about fifteen questions in a very serious tone without encouraging you or smiling at you. You cannot stop if you make a mistake. You have to work through the entire interview as if you were in front of your interview panel. Only after you're completely done can they offer you feedback.

To ensure the feedback they give will help, tell them to look for any weird nuances or habits you might have exhibited. Tell them to write down the numbers of any answers that were difficult for them to understand. If your answers are clear and organized, even someone not in your industry should be able to follow your thinking. If not, then you should revise the answer a bit.

Formally rehearsing in front of your friends and family can be even more nerve-wracking than interviewing with a bunch of people you don't know. This is why it's so helpful. If you treat it as a true dress rehearsal, at the real interview your brain will imagine you delivering that answer perfectly the day before, and you'll do even better.

Take the Shortcut

1. Memorize the main points you're going to use in each answer.
2. Practice answering each question out loud until your answers are perfectly clear and well organized.
3. Add a little flair to your interview by planning for some humor and for some unique or interesting thinking.
4. Do a dress rehearsal of the interview to help your brain rehearse what it will experience during the actual interview.

Chapter Six

Different Interview Formats

This chapter will describe different formats you might encounter when job interviewing. You won't always encounter interviews in the traditional face-to-face or panel format. Even in informal interactions, remember: you're always being interviewed and judged in some way. Make sure they judge you well.

You might have interactions with the person who schedules the interview, the people you see while in the waiting room, and the person at the other end of your emailed question. You must assume that all are providing input to the hiring manager. I've made decisions not to hire individuals before the person even walked into the panel, because the candidate was so rude to staff along the way.

No matter whom you interact with, you're being judged anytime you communicate with a member of the organization or the company. Be friendly, accommodating, and focused on excellence at all times.

Behavioral Event Interviews

The term behavioral event interview is utilized in a variety of ways. In the most scientific, pure form, it is a type of interview where the hiring manager asks you a very broad question. Then he probes your answer by following up on more specific questions. Any one question could be judging several of your traits or skills. In true behavioral event interviewing, the hiring manager is well trained. He will know the precise questions and follow-up questions which will be used, and under what conditions.

The theory behind behavioral event interviews is that they tend to level the playing field between those who are natural talkers and those who might be a little more reserved. In that sense, when done correctly, behavioral event interviewing can reduce bias by providing equal opportunities for individuals to share their thinking across cultural norms.

Behavioral event questions also focus on specific examples or events that have actually occurred. Interviewers using this strategy do not care about what you might do. They want to know about actual events that occurred. This allows the interviewer to probe the thinking behind why the candidate made certain decisions or took certain actions.

This method also allows interviewers to better gauge the candidate's level of actual work experience. The best predictor of future success is past success doing similar work. A vice president in one organization may not be doing the same strategy level work as a vice president in a different organization, even if the job titles are exactly the same.

Training hiring managers in the method behind behavioral event interviewing can be time consuming and expensive. For that reason, many organizations utilize behavioral event questions instead of conducting an entire behavioral event interview. Whenever the question is phrased with an introductory phrase similar to *Give us an example of a time when,* it is a clue to you that this is a behavioral event question.

The entire interview may be comprised of behavioral event questions. You'll know it's a behavioral event setting if the interviewer is constantly asking follow up questions such as:

What was the outcome? How did you decide to do _____?
What did you tell the group? What did you do next?

Here's an example to show how powerful behavioral event interview questions are in determining who has the right experience for the job. In two different positions I've held, I was required to fulfill multiple high-level management vacancies, all in the spring. We had many applicants aspiring to get into the hiring pool for consideration, and we needed to identify the top candidates for more in-depth interviews. Each February, we would conduct screening interviews. I always used the exact same three questions for the screening interviews, and only fifteen minutes was allotted per candidate.

Each question began as *Give us an example of a time when...* Needless to say, because the same three questions were used every year, candidates all knew what the questions would be. You would think that candidates would get better at answering the questions as time went on, since they all knew what they were. Surprisingly, that was not the case. Why? Because when you're asked to give a specific example of when you achieved certain results at work, and if you haven't achieved those results, it's nearly impossible to fake it!

Here are examples of behavioral event questions applicable to different job types: *Give me an example of a time when your colleagues told you something was impossible to do, but then you were able to do it. Give me an example of a time when you had to work with an individual or team who held opinions that were greatly different from your own. Give me an example of a time when you improved the culture where you worked.*

Regardless of how the entire interview is formatted, you can be sure you are going to get a few behavioral event questions. Below are my top tips for preparing to answer behavioral event interview questions.

44

1. Do your preparation homework and make sure you've memorized multiple examples of work outcomes you have accomplished. These can range from leading a team that delivered results on a big project to helping a coworker resolve a conflict with a customer.

2. When given the question, always describe the situation in detail. Be sure to explain what you did. Share what you were considering or thinking about when you did it. State why you eventually decided on a specific course of action. Conclude by describing what the end result was. Include pertinent details regarding how you handled difficult circumstances such as delays, roadblocks or personality differences.

3. End each question with a summary. Behavioral event questions are always successfully ended by you explaining what you learned from the experience or how you applied it in other settings.

Group Interviews

Group interviews are becoming more and more common. Companies usually use this format for line-level positions if they have a slate of multiple positions they need to fill at one time (such as a hotel or a store opening). Companies also use this technique when they want to see how the candidates interact with each other in a large group. In these instances, sometimes the company will give you a project or problem you need to work on together. Then they observe how you interact with others.

You should prepare for a group interview in the same way that you would prepare for a regular interview. You might not even know you're going to be in a group interview until you arrive. When you realize you're going to be in a group interview situation, prepare by reviewing these strategies to help you be successful.

1. Be poised. Don't get rattled by a group interview if you didn't anticipate one. When you walk in, smile and greet everyone and pretend like you're excited to have the group interview. This will help your mind also get ready for the process.

2. During the interview, one interviewer may not say anything and will just be taking notes, with no expression. Plan to make eye contact with that person just as if he is one of the main interviews, but don't get frazzled if the person doesn't respond.

3. During the interview, demonstrate that you are engaged and confident by sitting up straight, nodding, and smiling.

4. Be friendly. The company may be watching you interact with others before you even arrive. In addition, if you take the time to get to know your group, they are more likely to be thinking positive thoughts about you during the process. When you know their names, you can show personalized attention to them during the process by saying things like, "I loved what James just said, and I'd like to expand on that answer by saying..."

5. Be polite. Use your manners. Don't speak over people, and if you do accidentally interrupt, apologize. If you notice that one person in the group hasn't said anything, you can say, "I'd love to answer this question, but I feel like Ryan hasn't had a chance to speak yet, so I think I'll pass this to him." Every organization wants a good team player. Being polite and making sure to include everyone will impress the interviewers.

6. Be articulate. Use your memorized examples and answers just as if you were the only interviewee. However, you may need to shorten some of them to accommodate other group members. Thus, give the meat of your prepared answers but in a more succinct way, leaving out a few details.

The Coffee Chat Interview

As I said earlier, you are always being judged, no matter what venue you're sitting in. If you're with a company representative, formally or informally, you're in an interview. In determining if a candidate might fit into a team, often companies will schedule less formal interactions with potential coworkers. These occur over coffee, while touring the facility/location, or even in the car on the way to pick you up. Sometimes you're invited to have lunch or dinner.

Prepare for these informal interactions in much the same way as you would prepare for the formal interview. Individuals will ask you questions similar to what you've already heard, but they will ask them more informally. Make sure your answers are consistent throughout all of these interactions. I know candidates who made mistakes by more providing more details in these informal settings--details that were not helpful. I've also known candidates who demonstrated less than ideal personality traits when in an informal setting. Examples are being sarcastic, talking poorly about their former employer, and even using bad manners while eating.

Also prepare for these informal settings by having several questions to ask the person on hand, such as inquiring about the company and their role. If the potential coworker has to ask you all the questions, it could get awkward. So be sure to think about the flow of the conversation and how you will contribute to the back and forth. People love to talk about themselves.

Having questions handy like, *How long have you worked here?* and *What's your favorite thing about working here?* are good to elicit a positive response.

It's helpful in these situations to remember a few tips from psychology. First, how you make people feel is going to leave a stronger imprint in someone's memory that the details of what you said. So be sure that you bring up only positive topics that the person will feel proud to speak about or that will make him laugh or smile. Next, smile yourself as much as possible and appropriate. Your smile will leave a strong impression that you are a positive team player. Smiling also helps you be more relaxed.

Phone Interviews

Phone interviews are another way a future employer will get to know you. The typical purpose of a phone interview is to screen multiple candidates. The hiring manager will usually ask more in-depth questions regarding the work you have represented on your resume. Hiring managers receive a large number of resumes that are written very well. As a result, it becomes difficult to determine a highly experienced candidate from a less experienced one. To sort through many applicants who seem equally well-qualified on paper, phone screening interviews narrow down large pools of candidates. Employers then determine who will move on to an in-person interview.

There are several ways you can prepare for a phone interview. Most importantly, don't neglect to prepare, even if the recruiter states, "I just want to have a chat and ask you a few questions." It's not a chat. It's an interview and be sure to prepare as such. Also, if at all possible, make sure the hiring manager calls you on a landline so you don't run the risk of getting disconnected or having your answers fade in and out.

Next, unless it's an interview on Skype or FaceTime, the person can't see you, so have your notes and potential answers handy and accessible. It's best if you have them on notecards so that you don't make noise shuffling the papers around. But keep the conversation flowing. Don't pause after every question to give yourself time to locate the paper that has the answer on it.

Finally, put some personality into your interview. Keep your voice positive and upbeat, and engage in conversation before and after the phone interview. It's more difficult to make your personality shine over the phone. But you still want the hiring manager to view you as a friendly, collaborative future team member.

Take the Shortcut

1. There may be different formats, but you still need to prepare thoroughly for all of them.

2. Behavioral event interviews or questions require you to explain a work-related example in detail, including why you made certain decisions along the way.
3. Group interviews require you to be poised, friendly and a good team player in addition to being ready to answer questions.

4. You should prepare for informal meetings with potential coworkers just like you would prepare for the real interview, but come prepared with questions to ask in order to keep the dialogue flowing.

5. Get your notes gathered together and handy so that you can refer to them during a phone interview, but avoid being disruptive.

Chapter Seven

The McIntosh Fifteen

n this chapter, I have provided what I have found are the fifteen most common interview questions. I will give you methods to approach the answer and I will provide examples of good topics to cover. I will also explain the mistakes you should avoid making in your answer.

1. Tell us a little bit about yourself. This question comes in many forms, and is at the beginning of nearly every interview. Some companies will add to the beginning question "and why you want to work here" or "and your background and experiences that qualify you for position." No matter how the question is asked, be prepared to give a brief overview of your experience, tying that experience to the job qualifications. Then provide reasons why you are seeking that job, or seeking a new position. Close with what makes you excited about working for that specific company. This is the most important question because it's going to give the interview team their first impression of you. Because you know you're going to get the question, it should be perfectly delivered.

The most common mistake you can make is going into too much detail regarding experiences that are not relevant to the position. I've had to interrupt candidates and move on to question two, because, for example, they started by describing in detail their first leadership position as the student body president in sixth grade. If you're interviewing for your first job at the age of sixteen, that could be relevant. When you're forty years old, it's not. The further back the work experience, the less time you should spend on it. An exception would be if that is the only experience relevant to the position you're interviewing for.

In addition, unless your education or your specific university is vitally important to the position, you can skip over it in a few seconds, only mentioning that you received a degree. Plan to spend no more than five minutes on the first question, less if you're relatively new to your career.

2. *What is your biggest weakness?* The key to this question is not, as some say, turning your weakness into a strength. I have heard far too many versions of *I don't have great work-life balance because I work so much* or *Sometimes I can take on too much of a workload*. Make yourself stand out by having thought of a weakness in advance that is an actual area of growth for you. Plan also to explain how you have grown and improved in that area. That said, don't make the mistake of being too honest. If one of your weaknesses is that you have a hard time getting projects to completion, or you don't get along with coworkers, keep those to yourself. Safe topics include weaknesses such as getting distracted by your email in-box, controlling projects too much rather than letting others learn on their own, or not giving enough feedback.

3. *What is your biggest strength?* Don't pick any random strength. Choose a strength you have that is directly related to the job you're interviewing for. Be honest, but be smart about what strength you choose. The mistake people most often make on this question is choosing a strength that is only somewhat related to the job. If your greatest strength is that you get along well with your coworkers, and you'll be working alone in the job you're interviewing for, choose a more relevant strength.

4. *How would your friends/coworkers/last boss describe you?* Similar to the above, choose descriptors that are related to the job description. Unless the interviewer specifically asks you for something negative, focus on positive descriptors only.

51

Candidates fail to maximize this question when they choose descriptors that are positive, but not related to the position.

5. *Tell us about a mistake you've made and what you've learned from it.* Always be prepared for some version of this question by having in mind more than one option to use. At the interview, you can choose the option you haven't used in a previous example. The usual mistake candidates make on this question is overlapping the "weakness" question with an answer to this question. That's fine as long as you didn't mention the actual example in the weakness question. The other mistake candidates make is by not ending their answer to this question. They just describe the mistake without explaining how they learned from it. Be sure to provide a full answer by also explaining how you avoided making that same mistake in the future.

6. *Describe the type of supervision/boss that you most prefer.* The company wants to know if you'll fit in with your potential supervisor and the work environment. If you've done your homework, you know something about the culture at that company. You can tailor your answer to the type of supervision you would expect to receive at that company, but you should still be honest. Even though you really want the job, you don't want to work in an environment that doesn't match your style.

7. *What have you accomplished in your career that you are most proud of?* Try to find a larger project that you can explain in detail. Make sure that it is similar to the types of projects you would be doing in your new job. Frame your answer so that the interview panel understands why there was a need for what you did. Also detail the steps you took to accomplish the goal. Most importantly, state the end result and how it helped the organization.

You can make yourself stand out by using an example where you were very proud, yet didn't get to the full result you wanted. This helps you connect with the panel because most experienced professionals have had that happen at least once. Also, showing humility while still being proud of what you did accomplish can make a positive impact on the team. Candidates make mistakes on this question by describing something personal, such as *completing my degree* or *raising my three kids*. Those are certainly accomplishments to be proud of. However, remember that this is a job interview. You want to make your answer stand out from the others. Candidates also make a mistake if they use an example from many years back in their career. Interview panels want to know that you're constantly pushing yourself to do better. A recent accomplishment is more impactful than one that occurred several years ago.

8. *What has been the most difficult decision you've ever had to make?* This question is hard if you haven't thought of a difficult decision in advance, so be prepared with an example. It's best if the decision is related to a work problem. Consider answers when you had to make a decision where people, rather than profits, had to come first. For example, maybe you turned down a client because you thought their business model was less than ethical. Maybe you had to choose to get a deadline extension rather than force your assistant to work through the evening and miss her daughter's volleyball game. Maybe you chose to go the extra mile for a customer but had to explain to your boss why you had overtime that day.

When people haven't thought in advance about how to answer this question, they usually defer to a personal example. That is a mistake, and it rarely helps you get the job. If you can only think of a personal example, at least make it related to your career. One example would be turning down a job opportunity in another city because you didn't want to force your kids to switch high schools. Even so, be sure to explain well why the decision was difficult from a career perspective.

9. *Imagine your boss has made a decision or given you a directive that you don't agree with. How would you handle this situation?* Interview panels ask this question so often that candidates are almost always prepared for it. Therefore, most use the same answer. They explain all the ways they would try to convince their boss to make a different decision, but in the end, the boss is the boss. The candidate states that she would support the decision as if it were her own. That is the correct answer.

One way you can stand out from the crowd, however, is to offer a specific example. State what occurred and add in a strategy or technique that others may not have thought about. For example, maybe you were aware that your boss was under a lot of pressure and that's why she was making an ill-advised decision. You took her for lunch where she would be in a more relaxed setting and more willing to hear your reasoning. You could also give an example where you truly believed your boss was wrong, but she ended up being right. You learned from that experience to be more trusting of others' wisdom and experience.

Another way to be more unique than others is to provide more than one example, making the point that you know you need to differentiate your approach depending on your boss's style. This shows that you have depth of experience. It also shows that you think about how to approach a situation before acting. When people do make a mistake on this question, it's when they make comments about going over their boss's head. Unless the question specifically refers to a legal issue that would require reporting, always focus on how you would handle the situation directly with the boss, not with someone else.

10. *Give us an example of a time when you had to work with a group of coworkers who didn't have the same approach or work standards as you did. How did you handle the situation?* Be sure to explain the project's goals. Describe the differences

with your coworkers in a way that demonstrates you still valued their contributions. Describe specific strategies you used such as listening for understanding, clarifying, looking at it from their point of view, finding common ground between ideas, and adapting your style to match theirs.

Mistakes in this question usually occur in the descriptions of coworkers. When you describe your coworker differences in a negative way, it will make you look mean to the interview team. It may have been true that your coworker Stephen was an arrogant blowhard who always thought he was right. Instead of describing him that way, you should use other descriptors. You could say that Stephen had very strong beliefs, and needed a lot of facts and data before he would change his viewpoint.

Another mistake people make is by not providing specific strategies. They speak in vague terms, using phrases like *we worked it through* or *I just kept working at it until...* Make sure you have thought about very specific strategies you use when collaborating with coworkers. You can list the strategies in this question or similar questions that ask about your relationships with coworkers.

11. *Where do you see yourself/your career five to ten years from now?* This question is a tough one. You run the risk of sounding too arrogant, or even unrealistic, if you say, *I want to have your job five years from now.* On the other hand, you run the risk of sounding unambitious and possibly lazy if you say, *I just want to be doing well in this job ten years from now.* Some interview panels are actually looking for an ambitious go-getter. They might expect you to share really big expectations. Other interview panels want to see if your ambitions sound realistic relative to the job. They would be concerned if you're likely to jump ship for a better opportunity in another company.

Because you don't know how the panel might react, I recommend splitting the difference. It's usually safe to say that you are going to learn the new job for three to five years, and then look at opportunities to be challenged in a new position. You can make yourself stand out by outlining what you'll want to learn on the job each year. For example, you can say, *The first two years I really want to focus learning each revenue stream. Then I'd like to delve more deeply into mentoring others to reach their own potential.* There are a few exceptions to the above comments. If you're interviewing for a sales job, it's usually expected that you'll have big ambitions. You could say, *I hope by the end of five years, I would have reached $1 million in sales and grown my client base by 23%.*

If you're interviewing for a line-level position and don't plan to pursue higher-level positions, it's fine to indicate that. Just be sure to say why. It can be as simple as, *I'm not sure right now if I want to pursue leadership opportunities in the future. At this point I plan to focus on doing the best job for the company and for our customers.* If it's obvious you are at the tail end of your career due to your age, it's typically fine to say, *At this point in my career, I want to focus on one job where I can fully support my boss and coworkers in their endeavors. I want to help others so that they can reach their goals, by doing a great job myself. With my experience, I'd also like to mentor aspiring young workers and help them move up the ladder.*

12. *Tell us what we would see you doing the first 30, 60 and 90 days on the job.* Structure your answer so the interview panel understands you aren't going to jump in and change everything right away. You want them to know that you are going to observe and analyze before acting. Even if you know the company wants someone to come in and change everything, don't set yourself up for failure by promising to fix all problems in the first 90 days.

You should organize your answer by focusing on gathering data and developing relationships during the first 30 days. You can analyze and verify your assumptions within 60 days. Within

90 days, you can be beginning to get feedback on a draft action plan. As you describe each phase, give a short example of when you used that technique successfully in other job transitions, if you can. This is also a good question to weave in your background knowledge about the organization. Within each phase, you can comment on a relevant issue or concern you think may need to be handled. You could also mention the company's recent successes that you may be looking to build upon.

A mistake people make in this question is in assuming that there is something needing to be fixed by the time you get to an action plan. When you describe how you're approaching the situation, include an acknowledgement that if everything is working very well, you'll be looking for opportunities to improve, not only problems to fix. Another mistake people make is focusing only on the end result at 90 days, and not explaining different approaches being used in the first and second month. Whether the question is worded so that it only says 90 days, or only says within the first year, take a phased approach that will demonstrate your ability to be thoughtful about your actions.

13. *What do you do for fun outside of work, what hobbies do you have, and/or what was the last book you read?* There is usually a question that seeks to help the interview panel understand who you are as a person outside of work. Don't make up something that's not true. However, do use your background information to use something that matches the company culture or that is similar to an interest of one or more people on the interview team. (Reminder, you're not going to tell them you know it's something similar to what you discovered about them on Facebook, or you'll seem creepy). Safe topics include travel, working out, reading, coaching kids' sports/activities, photography, and the generic *spending time with family.*

If you have a unique hobby that might be funny or interesting to mention, it can help the interview team warm up to you. I had a candidate explain that she had recently gotten into disc golf. I had another candidate who had recently finished a ten-year quest to visit all 50 states on his motorcycle. One candidate volunteered frequently at an animal shelter.

Also try to come up with something interesting if they ask about what you have been reading. It's a great opportunity to stand out from the crowd, so make sure it's a book that might be unique from others. A leadership book is fine if it's all you've read recently, and feel free to mention it. But also try to find something different. Know that if they ask about the last book you've read, then it's clear reading is a value they hold. Be sure it's something other than what was required reading in college or that would be required of your career. It is also fine to mention novels, as long as you stick to best sellers and generally avoid mentioning any that might involve controversial topics.

14. *Is there anything we haven't asked you that you think is important for us to know, or is there anything you would like to add that you haven't yet talked about?* When asked this question, it means the interview is coming to an end. Always plan to have a perfect answer to this question, because you know you're going to get some version of it. It's your opportunity to give them a closing statement that impresses them and leaves them with a positive feeling about you as a coworker.

Do not use this question to talk about what you will gain from a career with the company. Instead, focus on what you will give the organization, and how you think you could add value to the team in achieving their goals. Explain how impressed you have been with their friendliness and their questions (or anything else that impressed you about the process). End by thanking them for their time and wishing them luck in finding the right candidate to meet their needs. You can say you hope it will be you, but also communicate your maturity by demonstrating understanding if it's not.

Many candidates make mistakes on this question. Some haven't prepared for it, so they decline to add anything. They have missed a big opportunity to end on a high note by selling themselves while further connecting to the interview panel. Other candidates make the mistake of being too pushy. They sell themselves, but they do so by sounding like arrogant know-it-alls. Their closing statement implies that the company would be stupid not to select them as the candidate. Some jobs (like sales jobs) may expect that type of confidence, but my experience is that it mostly rubs people the wrong way.

15. *Do you have any questions for us?* You should use this opportunity to ask interesting questions that might also show you have researched the company in some regard. There may be a new company initiative, a recent news story, or something you've observed or heard while researching the company. Use that information to frame a question at the end of the interview. Make sure it's the type of question that will make the interview team think. Also make sure your question isn't so difficult that it makes you sound like a pretentious know-it-all.

Some good questions are along the lines of, *What are some of the benefits you've seen so far regarding (x) initiative?* Another example is *I saw on the news that your company (did something great). What were some of the strategies you used to accomplish that goal?* It's a mistake to ask job benefit, salary, or process questions at this point in the interview. If you want to know more about the process beyond the panel interview, you can ask in a follow-up thank you email. Save salary and benefit questions for when and if you are offered the position. Your time with the interview team is precious. Maximize your chances of getting the job by ensuring your responses work to make you look polished, prepared, and professional.

Take the Shortcut

1. Prepare for these fifteen questions, and you will have a polished, practiced answer for the majority of interview questions you will receive.

2. Avoid the mistake of using personal examples instead of professional ones, even if the question is vague on which it is asking for.

3. Avoid the mistake of using any descriptors or examples that have the possibility of making you appear negative or arrogant.

4. Use different examples for each question, even if the questions are related.
5. Use the end of the interview to leave the interview panel with a polished, prepared and professional impression of you.

Chapter Eight

Would You Like More Help?

If you would like more extensive support for your job search via phone or in person, my husband and I own a small consulting company, Sensible Solutions. Among other resources, we provide career coaching services part-time to a limited number of individuals and groups. We work for an hourly rate outside our regular work hours, which usually means early mornings, evenings, and weekends. We also have several associates we think are fabulous and will refer you to them as well in the event our schedules are unable to accommodate your specific request. Just email me at stacimcintosh23@gmail.com if you're interested.

I also have other books providing guidance for you to succeed in every aspect of your job search and career. Check out my other books on Amazon if you want to learn more details about each aspect. Every book is short, will take you about an hour to read, and is packed with practical tips you can put into place immediately. All are published as part of the *One Hour Handbook Series*.

My other books focused on job success are currently available on Amazon in the Kindle store and in paperback form:
- *Job Search Passport: Using Industry Secrets to Write Applications, Resumes, and Cover Letters*
- *Wheels Up: Mastering the Job Interview to Launch Your Career*
- Coming soon: *Brace for Landing: Managing Your Life and Career After Being Laid-Off, Fired, Pushed Out or Demoted*
- Coming later: *Stuck In Coach: Promotion Strategies to Land a First Class Job*

If my advice in this book helped you, please do me a favor and take a few minutes to write an Amazon book review. My commitment to readers is that I will continue to write easy to read, accessible handbooks for those who don't have the time or money to invest in expensive books, personal coaching, or on-line courses to help their career. Reader reviews help sell books, and selling books allows me the opportunity to provide more job success content to an even broader audience.

Writing a review is easy to do. If you don't want to use your real name, you can easily adapt your existing Amazon account to create an anonymous Amazon public profile name. Whatever name you choose will be on the review. Reviews let other readers like you know how the book might help them. If you take the time to write a review, I will gladly put you on my mailing list to receive free advance copies of new handbooks before they are available to the public.

Chapter Nine

No Regrets

One of my most trusted mentors is a woman by the name of Barb Wright. Barb hired me into human resources without any experience, and she took the time to train me over ten years. At the heart of it, she is the reason I am able to write this book today. When she retired, I was hired to be Barb's replacement. Extremely wise, Barb always advised people to think, *Thank you for hiring me. Thank you for not hiring me.* The point was, if you give it your all and they still don't hire you, then you just aren't a match for that organization. Which means you wouldn't have been happy working there anyway. When you have no regrets about how you performed in the interview, it's easy to be at peace thinking to yourself, *It's their loss!*

My hope for you after your interview is that you have no regrets. I love to hear the experiences of my readers! Please share your No Regrets story by emailing me at stacimcintosh23@gmail.com or by posting your experience on my Facebook page @McIntoshBooks. Also feel free to email me if you have a question or if you want to give me suggestions for new content. You can also pay it forward and inspire others by sharing your No Regrets story as part of your Amazon book review. Experience is the best teacher, so I may use your story in future editions of this book!

Staci McIntosh can be contacted via the following:

Email: stacimcintosh23@gmail.com
Facebook: @McIntoshBooks
Twitter: @StaciVegas

I very much appreciate you taking the time to write an Amazon book review.

Made in the USA
Middletown, DE
25 October 2017